Joke
Book

Nestlé®

smarties®

Joke

Book

Edited by Justin F. Scroggie
Illustrations by David Mostyn

Robinson Children's Books

Constable & Robinson Ltd
3 The Lanchesters
162 Fulham Palace Road
London W6 9ER
www.constablerobinson.com

First published in the UK by Robinson Children's Books,
an imprint of Constable & Robinson Publishing Ltd, 1999

A copy of the British Library Cataloguing in Publication Data for this title
is available from the British Library.

ISBN 1 - 84119 - 069 - 1

Printed and bound in the EC

10 9

CONTENTS

INTR●●-II- TI●N

What do you call a kid with 200 **smarties**? *Popular!*

What do you call a kid with 200 **smarties** <u>and</u> a joke for every **smarties**? *Even more popular!*

Welcome to the smarties JOKE BOOK, a gigantic collection of jokes specially designed to dazzle your friends, disarm your enemies, impress your brothers or sisters and irritate your parents (and other very old people).

You'll find jokes in here of all shapes and sizes. There are DOCTOR DOCTOR jokes (who *is* this doctor, and why are there always two of them?) There are KNOCK KNOCK jokes (funny, you never hear any doorbell jokes, do you?) There are WAITER WAITER jokes (it must be the worst restaurant in the world!), as well as MAD and FRUITY jokes, TEACHER and VAMPIRE jokes, DINOSAUR and BUG jokes, and lots of other gags and giggles. There's even a special section just for jokes about smarties!

Remember: there are lots of different ways of laughing at these jokes. You can laugh like a HYENA or like a DRAIN. You can laugh your HEAD OFF and split your SIDES at the same time (messy). You can laugh up your SLEEVE, or on the other side of your FACE. You can laugh and the WHOLE WORLD will laugh with you. You can even have the LAST LAUGH!

But one thing's guaranteed. YOU WILL LAUGH!

WATCH ME MOVE AND GROW! HOLD THE BOOK FIRMLY IN YOUR RIGHT HAND AND FLICK THE PAGES QUICKLY STARTING AT THE BACK.

Smartie Pant

Why are chocolate buttons rude? Because they look like Smarties in the nude.

What's the difference between Smarties and Santa Claus? Santa Claus comes round once a year, Smarties are round all the time.

Why did the vampire eat the red Smartie? He thought it was a blood blister.

What do you call a Smartie with an electric guitar? Chock Berry.

What is a Smartie's favourite instrument?
The Tuba.

What do you call a policeman with a red Smartie, a yellow Smartie and a green Smartie on his head?
A traffic cop.

What is the cleverest letter of the alphabet?
Smart E.

What do you call a dog that has Smarties every morning for breakfast?
Lucky.

When does a Smartie sit on a sofa?
When it's a three-piece sweet.

How can you tell when a
Smartie-eater is angry?
He keeps flipping his lid.

Waiter, waiter, there's a Smartie in my cocktail!
It's a Smartini, sir.

What do you call a green Smartie with yellow dots and fur on?
Old.

12

Why did the ant run away from the Smartie?
It thought it was a flying saucer.

What do you call a Smartie with a large dog?
Sir.

Doctor, doctor. I think I'm a tube of Smarties.
It's probably contagious.
How can you tell?
You've just given some to me.

What's a Smartie's favourite quote from Shakespeare?
Tubey or not tubey.

What do you get if you cross a
Smartie with a spell?
A Magic Circle.

What do you call a Smartie in a
combine harvester?
Shredded Sweet.

Why did the Smartie
cross the road?
To get to the tube.

What's the difference between a
brown Smartie and a slug?
What d'you mean, you don't know?

What's round, multi-coloured and keeps throwing up?
A packet of Smarties in a tennis-ball machine.

What do you call a large van full of Smarties?
A Smarticulated lorry.

Why did Frank Bruno put Smarties in his gloves?
He wanted to chocolate-box.

What kind of rice comes in a tube?
Bas-Smartie Rice.

**Which Smartie went Back to the Future?
Smarty McFly.**

**What do you get if you cross a sweet with a fish?
A Smart Eel.**

Why did the sweety wear a jacket and tie? He wanted to look Smarty.

What do you call a very old Smartie? A Smartefact.

Which Smartie is like a book?
The red one.

Which Smarties were in "Star Wars"?
Smar2D2 and Tube Acca.

Teacher: Suppose you
30 children had 6
Smarties each, and I
took 4 Smarties away
from each of you.
What would I have?
Class: A riot, Miss.

Did you hear about the man who
covered his walls in coloured patterns
made out of Smarties?
He called it
"Smart Deco"!

What do you call a boy with a tube full of orange Smarties?
Lucky.

What do you eat fake Smarties with?
False teeth, of course.

Three Smarties were having a game of golf. Where did the two blue ones play?
On the green.

Why did the elephant
paint his toenails red,
his trunk green and his
ears blue?
So he could hide in a
tube of Smarties.

What do you call a school outing
travelling on the underground?
A tube of Smarties.

What do you call a
clever dinosaur?
A Smartosaurus.

What do you call a white Smartie?
Secondhand.

Why did the dog throw his Smarties out of the window?
He wanted chocolate drops.

What's the difference between yellow Smarties and blue Smarties?
"Yellow Smarties" has more letters.

A man walks into a shop with his grizzling son. The kind shopkeeper says: "How about some Smarties for the kid?" The man replies: "Seems like a fair swap."

Bugs Funnies

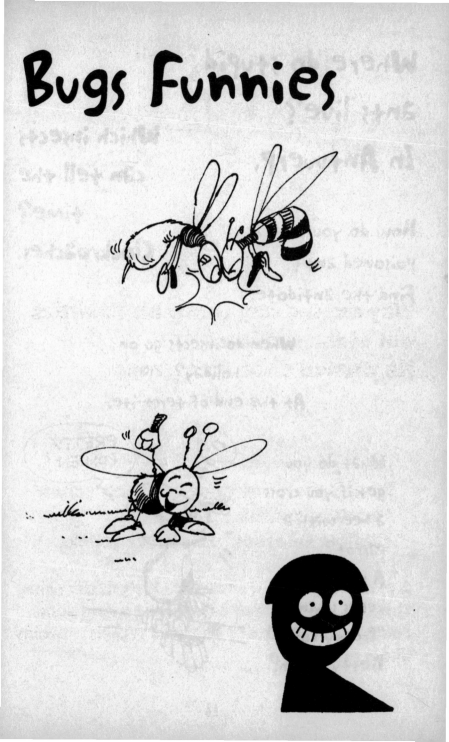

Where do stupid ants live?
In Antwerp.

Which insects can tell the time?
Clockroaches.

How do you cure a poisoned ant?
Find the antidote.

When do insects go on holiday?
At the end of term-ite.

What do you get if you cross a bee with a parrot?
A bird that keeps saying "Pretty Pollen! Pretty Pollen!"

PRETTY POLLEN!

What do you get if you cross a mosquito with a knight?
A bite in shining armour.

What did the termite say when he saw that his friends had completely eaten a chair?
"Wooden you know it!"

Why did the firefly keep stealing things?
He was light-fingered.

Which fly captured the ladybird?
The dragonfly.

What goes "snap, crackle, pop"?
.. firefly with a short circuit.

How do fireflies start a race?
Ready, steady, glow!

What has six
legs, bites and
talks in code?
.. morse-quito.

What is small
and grey, sucks
blood and eats
cheese?
A mouse-quito.

Why are mosquitoes annoying?
Because they get under your skin.

What is a mosquito's favourite sport?
Skin diving.

What do you call an insect that has
just flown by?
A flu bug.

Why do we know that insects have
amazing brains?
Because they always know when
you're having a picnic.

What do you call a top pop group
made up of nits?
The Lice Girls.

What car do insects
drive?
A Volkswagen
Beetle.

What do you get
if you cross a
praying mantis
with a termite?
A bug that says
grace before
eating your house.

What insect can fly
underwater?
A bluebottle in
a submarine.

What
lies down
a
hundred
feet in
the air?
A
centipede.

Why is the
letter 't' so
important
to a stick
insect?
Without it, it
would be
a sick insect.

What do you call a
musical insect?
A humbug.

HHUUUMMM

What's the difference between a maggot
and a cockroach?
Cockroaches crunch more when you eat
them.

Why was the insect kicked out of
the park?
It was a litterbug.

What do you call a
mosquito on holiday?
An itch-hiker.

What do you get if you cross Zorro
with an insect?
The Masked-quito.

What has antlers and sucks your blood?
A moose-quito.

What do insects learn at school?
Mothematics.

How can you make a moth ball?
Hit it with a fly swatter.

What is a myth?
A female moth.

"Why would" they let the butterfly
into the dance?
Because it was a moth ball.

What is the
biggest moth?
A mam-moth.

That do bees do if they want
to use public transport?
Wait at a buzz stop.

How does a queen bee
get around the hive?
She's throne.

What's yellow and brown and covered
in blackberries?
A bramble bee.

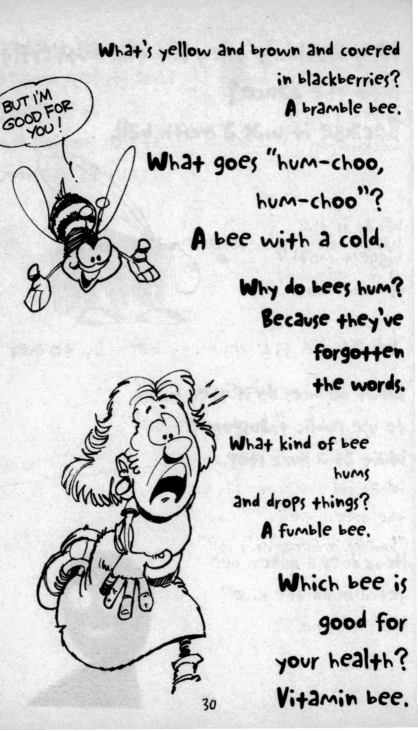

BUT I'M GOOD FOR YOU!

What goes "hum-choo,
hum-choo"?
A bee with a cold.

Why do bees hum?
Because they've
forgotten
the words.

What kind of bee
hums
and drops things?
A fumble bee.

Which bee is
good for
your health?
Vitamin bee.

What goes zzub, zzub? A bee flying backwards.

Why did the bee have its legs crossed as it flew? It was looking for the BP station.

What bee can never be understood?
A mumble-bee.

What did the mummy bee say to her naughty son?
"Just beehive!"

What did the drone say to the queen bee?
"Swarm in here, isn't it?"

What is the bees' favourite TV channel?
The Bee Bee C.

What do you get
if you cross a
bee with a door-
bell?
A hum-dinger.

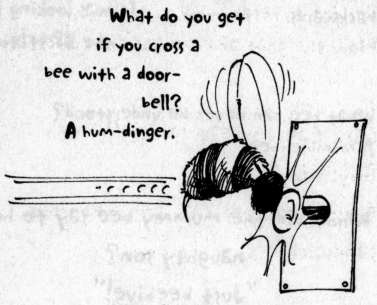

Why do bees have sticky hair?
Because of the honey combs.

Where do wasps come from?
Stingapore.

Where do you take a sick wasp?
To waspital.

While visiting close friends, a gnat,
Decided to sleep in a hat.
But an elderly guest
Decided to rest.
Now the gnat and the hat are quite flat.

Girl: Can you eat spiders?
Boy: Why?
Girl: One's just crawled into your
sandwich.

Father: Why did you put a toad in your
sister's bed?
Son: I couldn't find a spider.

Did you hear about the bloke who set up a flea circus?
He started it from scratch.

What medicine do you give a sick ant?
Antibiotics.

What do you call an ant with five pairs of eyes?
Ant-ten-eye

What do you call an 80-year-old ant?
An antique.

What's the biggest ant in the world?
An eleph-ant

What is even bigger than that?
A Gi-ant.

What do you call a spider wearing glasses? Sixteen-Eyes.

What's a spider's favourite takeaway? Chicken Buggets.

What do spiders sing at football matches? "We're on our way to Webley."

What do earwigs sing at football matches? Ear we go. Ear we go. Ear we go.

How many ants are needed to fill
an apartment?
Ten-ants.

Where do posh ants
eat?
In a restaur-ant.

What has 50 legs but
can't walk?
Half a centipede.

Why did the
insects drop the
centipede from
their football
team?
It took him too
long to put his
boots on.

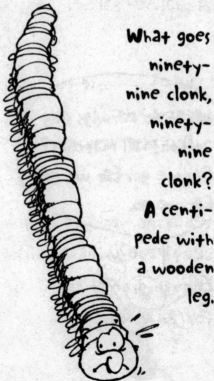

What goes
ninety-
nine clonk,
ninety-
nine
clonk?
A centi-
pede with
a wooden
leg.

What do you call a guard
with 100 legs?
A sentrypede.

What do you get if you cross a
centipede with a parrot?
A walkie-talkie.

What is worse than a crocodile with
toothache?
A centipede with athlete's foot.

What do you get if you cross a
centipede with a chicken?
Enough drumsticks
for an army.

What do you get if you cross a
tarantula with a rose?
I don't know, but I wouldn't try
smelling one!

What happened when the
chef found a daddy-long-
legs in the lettuce?
The insect became daddy-
short-legs.

How do
you know
if a spider
is with
it?
He
doesn't
have a
web, he
has
a website.

Why did the spider
buy a car?
He wanted to take
it out for a spin.

What does a
spider do when
he gets angry?
He goes up the
wall.

What has eight legs and lives in trees?
Four anti-road protestors.

What kind of doctors are spiders like?
Spin doctors.

What do you call a hundred spiders on a tyre?
A spinning wheel.

What did the spiders say to the fly?
"We're getting married. Do you want to come to the webbing?"

What does a cat go to sleep on?
A caterpillar.

What's green
and
dangerous?
A caterpillar
with a hand
grenade.

What does a caterpillar do on New Year's Day?
Turns over a new leaf.

What's the definition of a caterpillar?
A worm in a fur coat.

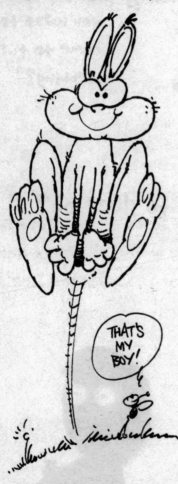

THAT'S MY BOY!

What is green and can jump a mile a minute?
A grasshopper with hiccoughs.

Why is it better to be a grasshopper than a cricket?
Because grasshoppers can play cricket, but there's no such game as "grasshopper".

What do you get if you cross a flea with a rabbit?
A bug's bunny.

How do you start an insect race?
One, two, flea, go!

What's the difference between a flea and a coyote?
One prowls on the hairy, the other howls on the prairie.

What did one flea say to another after a night out?
"Shall we walk home or take a dog?"

Two fleas were running across the top of a packet of soap powder.
"Why are we running so fast?" gasped one.
"Because it says 'Tear Along the Dotted Line'."

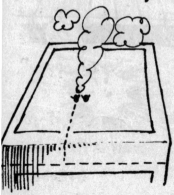

What do you call a cheerful flea?
A hop-timist.

Two fleas were sitting on Robinson Crusoe's back. One hopped off saying, "Byee! See you on Friday!"

Two mosquitoes were buzzing round when they saw a drunken man. One said to the other, "You bite him – I'm driving."

A flea jumped over the swinging doors of a saloon, drank three whiskeys and jumped out again. He picked himself up from the dirt, dusted himself down and said, "OK, who moved my dog?"

Two spiders were sitting on a web. One of them said, "See that fly up there? He's never flown before."
The other one said, "What's that got to do with you?"
The first one said, "I'm trying to talk him down."

Why did the flea fail his exams?
He wasn't up to scratch.

Little Miss
Muffet
Sat on a tuffet
Eating a bowl of stew.
Along came a spider
And sat down beside her.
Guess what? She ate
him up, too!

What's the best way to avoid being troubled by biting insects? Don't bite any!

Two caterpillars were crawling along a twig when a butterfly flew by.
"You know," said one caterpillar to the other, "when I grow up, you'll never get me in one of those things."

Doctor, doctor, a cockroach bit me.
Don't worry, it's just a nasty bug that is going round.

How do nits go on holidays?
British Hairways.

Mrs Smith: Is that fishmonger in the High Street any good?
Mrs Brown: He must be – 10,000 flies can't all be wrong!

Lights On,
Nobody Home

HEE HE HE !!!

What's mad, has six legs
and lives on the moon?
A Lunar-tic.

**She's so stupid, she thinks an
omelette is a small "om".**

Did you hear about
the mad superhero?
He flies like a spider, sees
like a bat and wears his
pants on the inside.

Why are phone operators mad?
Because they keep hearing voices.

He's so stupid he thinks an estate agent is a spy with a long car.

Why wouldn't the crazy astronaut go to the moon?
He said it would cost the earth.

My sister's so stupid she thinks a karaoke is a man who delivers trees.

Why did the stupid man buy a chess set?
He was saving it for a brainy day.

What's more dangerous
than fooling with bee?
Being with a fool.

What do crazy worms sing?
Mad-wriggles.

How do you get a mad-man to open up?
Use a nutcracker.

What do you call a mad young octopus?
A crazy, mixed-up squid.

Why are vampires crazy?
Because they're often bats.

Did you hear about the man who stole some rhubarb?
He was put into custardy.

Eddy's father called up to him, "Eddy, if you don't stop playing that trumpet, I think I'll go crazy." "I think you are already," replied Eddy, "I stopped playing half an hour ago."

What did they call the crazy golfer?
A crack putt!

What's brown and mad and lives in South America? A Brazil nut.

What do you get if you cross a witch with a werewolf?
A mad dog that chases aeroplanes.

Did you hear about the mad scientist who put dynamite in his fridge? They say he blew his cool.

Did you hear about the mad scientist who invented a gas so strong it burns its way through anything?
No, what about him?
Now he's trying to invent something to keep it in!

What's the difference between head lice and nits?
A real nit is too stupid to find your head.

Why did the stupid witch keep her clothes in the fridge?
She liked to have something cool to slip into in the evening.

What did the stupid ghost do?
He used to climb over walls.

What happened to the stupid wizard who put his false teeth in the wrong way round? He ate himself.

What do you call a stupid skeleton? Bonehead.

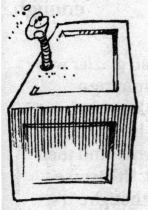

Did you hear about the stupid woodworm? He was found in a brick.

Did you hear about the stupid jellyfish? It set!

Did you hear about the stupid wizard? He couldn't remember if he used to be forgetful.

Why is the crazy red-headed boy like a biscuit?
Because he's a ginger nut.

Why did the crazy person give up his attempt to cross the Channel on a plank? He couldn't find a plank that was long enough.

A mad glazier was examining a broken window. He looked at it for a while and then said, "It's worse than I thought. It's broken on both sides."

Why do crazy people eat biscuits? Because they're crackers.

My mother is so stupid that she thinks a string quartet is four people playing tennis.

My friend is so stupid that he thinks twice before saying nothing.

Why did the stupid sailor grab a bar of soap when his ship sank? He thought he could wash himself ashore.

A stupid bank robber rushed into a bank, pointed two fingers at the clerk and said, "This is a muck-up."
"Don't you mean a stick-up?" asked the girl.
"No," said the robber, "it's a muck-up. I've forgotten my gun."

A stupid man spent the evening with some friends, but when the time came for him to leave, a terrific storm started with thunder, lightning and torrential rain.
"You can't go home in this," said the host, "you'd better stay the night."
"That's very kind of you," said the man. "I'll just pop home and get my pyjamas."

Did you hear about the stupid Australian who got a new boomerang for his birthday?
He spent two days trying to throw the old one away.

The stupid monster went to the mind-reader's and paid £5 to have his thoughts read.
After half an hour the mind-reader gave him his money back.

What did the stupid ghost call his pet zebra?
Spot.

**Did you hear about the stupid
sports fan who listened to a match?
He burned his ear!**

Did you hear about the stupid photographer?
He saved burned-out light bulbs for use in his
darkroom.

Did you hear about the stupid
monster who hurt himself while
he was raking up leaves?
He fell out of the tree.

Why did the stupid pilot land his
plane on the house?
Because the landing
lights were on.

Did you hear about the stupid water polo player? His horse drowned...

Why did the stupid racing driver make ten pit stops during the Grand Prix? He was asking for directions.

Did you hear about the stupid tap dancer? He fell in the sink.

The criminal mastermind found one of his gang sawing the legs off his bed. "What are you doing that for?" demanded the crook boss.
"You told me to lie low for a bit!" said the stupid thug.

What's red and grows in an
orange tree?
A stupid strawberry.

**He's so stupid he
couldn't spell "Anna"
backwards.**

JEMIMA: Remember I'm a big name in
these parts.
JONATHAN: Yes, THICK AND STUPID is
quite a mouthful.

BOSS: Why do you want a day off next week?
BRIAN: To get married, sir.
BOSS: Get married? What woman would be
stupid enough to marry you?
BRIAN: Your daughter, sir.

That builder's so stupid he's got a notice saying "Stop" on the top of his ladder.

This morning my dad gave me soap flakes instead of corn flakes for breakfast!
I bet you were mad.
Mad? I was foaming at the mouth!

Mum: Peter! Why are you scratching yourself?
Peter: 'Cos no one else knows where I itch.

**Why did the crazy professor wear a lifejacket at night?
Because he liked sleeping on a water bed, and couldn't swim!**

Doctor, Doctor

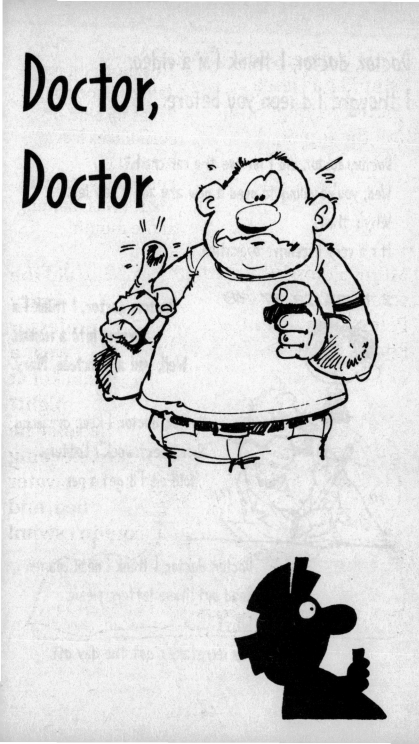

Doctor, doctor, I think I'm a video.
I thought I'd seen you before.

Doctor, doctor, did I survive the car crash?
Well, you're going to need a new arm and a new leg.
Why's that?
It's a very expensive operation.

2 16 23 29 37 38

Doctor, doctor, I think I'm
turning into a woman.
Well, you are sixteen, Mary.

Doctor, doctor, I keep dreaming
about next week's Lottery.
Hold on, I'll get a pen.

Doctor, doctor, I think I need glasses.
Read out these letters, please.
Why?
My secretary's got the day off.

Doctor, doctor, I keep thinking I'm a yo-yo.
– How are you feeling?
Oh, up and down.

Doctor, doctor, my son has a nail-biting problem.
– Is it serious?
Well, they're not his nails.

Doctor, doctor, I've got holes all over my body.
I'm not surprised, I'm an acupuncturist.

Doctor, doctor, I feel like going
on a long holiday.
– Take these.
What are they?
– My kids.

Doctor, doctor, I
keep feeling sick.
– How bad is it?
Well, it's not my sick.

Monster: Doctor, doctor, how do I stop my nose from running?
Doctor: Stick out your foot and trip it up.

Doctor, doctor, I'm so ugly. What can I do about it? Hire yourself out for Hallowe'en parties.

FOR HIRE

Doctor, doctor, I'm having difficulty sleeping.
Well maybe it's your bed.
Oh, I'm all right at night, it's during the day I have problems.

Patient: Doctor, doctor, I feel terrible. I can hardly breathe, I can't walk, I keep having palpitations and my skin is covered in nasty blotches.
Doctor: Oh, dear.
Patient: Are you writing me a prescription?
Doctor: No, a note for the undertaker.

Doctor, doctor, I tend to flush a lot.
Don't worry, that's just a chain reaction.

Doctor, doctor, I think I'm losing my memory.
When did this happen?
When did what happen?

Monster: Doctor, doctor, I need to lose 30 pounds of excess flab.
Doctor: All right, I'll cut your head off.

Monster: Doctor, doctor, I think I'm a bridge.
Doctor: What on earth's come over you?
Monster: Six cars, two trucks and a bus.

Wizard: Doctor, doctor, have you worked out what's the matter with me?
Doctor: I just don't know. It must be the drink.
Wizard: All right, I'll come back when you're sober.

Doctor, doctor, I keep thinking I'm a slice of bread.
You've got to stop loafing around.

Doctor, doctor, I keep thinking I'm a moth.
So why did you come to see me?
Well, I saw the light in the window ...

Doctor, doctor, I keep thinking I'm a python.
Oh, you can't get round me like that, you know.

Doctor, doctor, I'm a blood-sucking monster
and I keep needing to eat doctors.
Oh, what a shame. I'm a dentist.

Monster: Doctor, doctor, how long can one live without a brain?
Doctor: That depends. How old are you?

Doctor, doctor, there's an invisible man in the waiting room.
Tell him I can't see him without an appointment.

Witch: Doctor, doctor, I keep thinking I'm my
own cat.
Doctor: How long have you
thought this?
Witch: Since I was
a kitten.

Doctor, doctor, I keep thinking
I'm an elastic band.
Stretch yourself out on the couch.

Doctor, doctor, I snore so
loudly I keep myself awake!
Sleep in another room then.

Doctor, doctor,
I've got a
split personality.
Sit down, both
of you.

Doctor, doctor, I keep thinking you're
a vampire.
Necks, please!

Doctor, doctor, I swallowed
a skeleton's bone.
Are you choking?
No, I'm serious.

BLUD

Doctor, doctor, I keep thinking I'm a toad.
Go on, hop it!

Doctor, doctor, every night I
dream there are a thousand witches
under my bed. What can I do?
Saw the legs off your bed.

Doctor, doctor, I keep thinking I'm a snail.
Don't worry, we'll soon have
you out of your shell.

Doctor, doctor,
what would you
take for this
cold?
Make me an
offer.

Doctor, doctor, I've broken my arm
in two places.
Well, don't go back to those
places again.

Doctor, doctor, I think I'm a spoon.
Sit over there, please, and don't stir.

Doctor, doctor, I think I'm Napoleon.
How long have you felt like this?
Ever since Waterloo.

Doctor, doctor, how can I stop my cold going to
my chest?
Tie a knot in your neck.

Doctor, doctor, my left leg is giving me a lot of pain.
I expect that's old age.
But my right leg is as old, and that doesn't
hurt at all!

68

Doctor, doctor, my wife thinks she's a duck.
You'd better bring her in to see me straight away.
I can't do that – she's already flown south for the winter.

Doctor, doctor, I've just swallowed the film from my camera.
Well, let's hope nothing develops.

Doctor, doctor, I'm really worried
about my breathing.
Don't be – we'll soon find
something
to stop it.

Doctor, doctor, I
keep seeing double.
Take a seat, please.
Which one?

Doctor, doctor, I think I've been bitten by a vampire.
Drink this glass of water.
Will it make me better?
No, but I'll be able to see if your neck leaks.

Doctor, doctor, I keep thinking I'm a pair of curtains!
Pull yourself together, man.

Doctor, doctor, I've got a little sty.
Then you'd better buy a little pig.

Doctor, doctor, I'm nervous, this is the first brain
operation I've had.
Don't worry, it's the first I've performed.

Doctor, doctor, I've got carrots growing out of my ears!
How on earth did that happen?
I don't know. I planted cucumbers.

Doctor, doctor, my brother thinks he is a piece of chewing gum.
Well, send him to see me.
I can't. He's stuck under the table.

Doctor, doctor, I keep thinking
I'm a caterpillar.
Don't worry, you'll soon change.

Doctor, doctor, my sisters think I'm mad because I like peas.
There's nothing wrong with that, I like peas, too.
Oh, good, come back to my hovel, and
I'll show you my collection.

Doctor, doctor! I feel like a
sheep!
That's baaaaaad!

Doctor, doctor, my brother smells like a fish.
Poor sole!

Doctor, doctor, I've had tummy ache since I
ate three crabs yesterday.
Did they smell bad when you took them out of
their shells?
What do you mean "took them
out of their shells"?

Doctor, doctor! You've taken out my tonsils, my adenoids, my
gall bladder, my varicose veins and my appendix,
but I still don't feel well.
That's quite enough out of you.

Doctor,
doctor! I
think I need
glasses!
You
certainly
do, madam.
This is a
fish and
chip shop.

Jurassic Jokes

Why are dinosaurs great at parties?
They always raise the roof.

What is the dinosaurs' favourite TV show?
The X-tinct Files.

What do you get if you
cross a bouncy castle with
a dinosaur?
A sore bottom.

What do you call a dinosaur
waterproof jacket?
A Big Top.

Why did the dinosaur sleep
under the oil tank?
Because he wanted to get
up oily.

What do dinosaurs put
on their chips?
Tomatosaurus.

What do you call a clever dinosaur?
Lonely.

How do dinosaurs eat vegetables?
One farm at a time.

Why did the dinosaur cross the road?
What road?

What do you
get if you
cross a
dinosaur
with a CD-
Rom?
A mega-bite.

Why did the dinosaurs become extinct?
They took up hang-gliding.

What do you call a group of people
who dig for fossils?
A skeleton crew.

Nik: Whats the
difference between a
lemon, a dinosaur and a
tube of glue?
Tom: You can squeeze a
lemon, but you can't
squeeze a dinosaur. But
what about the tube of
glue?
Nik: Ha! I thought
that's where
you'd get stuck.

What do you get when a dinosaur skydives?
A large hole.

What do you call a prehistoric animal the day after it has done too much exercise?
A dino-sore.

How late do dinosaurs sleep in the morning?
As late as they want.

Which dinosaur has four legs and flies?
A dead one.

What is very heavy, has a long neck and cuts
through wood?
A dino-saw.

What's very heavy, has a long neck
and goes "ka-boom"?
Dino-mite.

What do you call a
dinosaur covered in leaves?
A Treeceratops.

What do you call a dinosaur that steps on
everything in its way?
Tyrannosaurus Wrecks.

What do call a dinosaur who wades
around in the mud?
A brown-toesaurus.

What's the scariest dinosaur of them all?
A terrordactyl.

How can you call a
Tyrannosaurus a light eater?
Because as soon as it gets light it
starts to eat.

What kind of dinosaurs know
how to use computers?
Trilo-bytes.

What has a spiked tail, plates on its back, and wheels?
A stegosaurus on roller blades.

What do you call a 65 million-year-old dinosaur?
A fossil.

What's worse then seeing a
dinosaur's teeth?
Seeing its tonsils.

What is the name of the
most famous dinosaur
authors?
The Bronto sisters.

How do you get down from a
dinosaur?
You don't, down comes
from a duck.

What do you call a
skinny dinosaur?
A stickosaurus.

What did dinosaurs put on their
floors?
Rep-tiles.

What did the dinosaur eat after
having his teeth out?
The dentist.

What do you get if you cross a dog
with a dinosaur?
A nervous postman.

How many dinosaurs had one leg?
All of them.

What do you get if you give a dinosaur a
pogo stick?
Big holes in your driveway.

Why doesn't the dinosaur like to play
on a swing?
He prefers the
see-saurus.

How do you take a Brontosaurus's temperature?
With a very long thermometer.

Where are dinosaurs buried?
In the ground.

Henry: Can you spell "blind dinosaur"?
Nik: B-L-I-N-D D-I-N-O-S-A-U-R.
Henry: Wrong - if it had two 'i's', it wouldn't be blind.

What's the cheapest way to hire a dinosaur?
Put bricks under its feet.

 How do dinosaurs kiss?
With their lips, silly!

What's big and fierce and is worn around your neck?
A tie-rannousarus.

What's as big as a dinosaur but doesn't weigh anything?
The dinosaur's shadow.

Why did the dinosaur raise one leg as it ate? If it raised two it'd fall over!

What did the Triceratops wear on its legs?
Tricerabottoms.

Two dinosaurs met in a revolving door.
They've been going round together ever
since.

What do you do with a green dinosaur?
Wait until it ripens.

How much did the dinosaur have to pay
the psychiatrist?
Not much for the hour of counselling,
but lots for the couch.

Why did the dinosaur cross
the road?
Because in those days they
didn't have chickens.

Tim: I can lift a dinosaur with one hand.
Joey: That's impossible.
Tim: Show me a dinosaur with one hand and I'll
prove it.

What do you have if you cross a dinosaur with
a vampire?
A blood shortage.

What is the best way to speak
to a dinosaur?
Long-distance.

What do you do with a blue dinosaur?
Cheer him up.

What did the Loch Ness Monster say to the dinosaur?
Long time no sea.

What's the hardest part of making dinosaur soup?
Stirring it.

What did the love-struck dinosaur say to the grand piano?
"Darling, what lovely teeth."

How do you know if there's a dinosaur in your bath?
You can't get the shower curtain closed.

Did you hear about the Tyrannosaurus twins?
They were both called Rex.

Why did the dinosaur jump up and down?
Because he'd just taken his medicine but he'd forgotten to shake the bottle.

What happened to Ray when he met the velociraptor?
He became an ex-Ray.

Why are most dinosaurs covered in wrinkles?
Have you ever tried to iron a dinosaur?

Why did the dinosaur walk over the hill?
It was too much bother to walk under it.

Why did the dinosaur drink ten litres of antifreeze?
So he didn't have to buy a winter coat.

Why do dinosaurs wear glasses?
So they don't bump into other dinosaurs.

Gag the Teachers!

Teacher: Why are you late for school, Billy?
Billy: My Dad brought me in the car.
Teacher: Was the traffic bad?
Billy: No, my Dad can't drive.

Head: This is your new class, Mr Best, you'll
find the children very friendly.
Mr Best: Where do I sit?
Head: In the bunker over there.

Sally: I just love History.
Anne: Why's that?
Sally: So many dates!

Boy: Miss, Johnny keeps looking at my answers!
Teacher: Don't worry, he won't find anything.

Why did the teacher decide to become an electrician?
To get a bit of light relief.

Teacher: Who can tell me what "dogma" means?
Cheeky Charlie: It's a lady dog that's had puppies, Sir.

Did you hear about the man who took up monster-baiting for a living?
He used to be a teacher but he lost his nerve.

"Don't worry Miss Jones," said the headmaster to the new teacher. "You'll cope with your new class, but they'll keep you on your toes."
"How's that, Sir?" asked the teacher.
"They put drawing pins on the chairs."

What's the difference between a railway guard and a teacher?
One minds the train, the other trains the mind.

"I see you've got that new boy down for the football game against Brick Street," said the English teacher to the games master.
"Yes, but I'm not sure what position to play him."
"Well, if his football's anything like his English, he's a natural drawback."

Why did the singing teacher have such a high-pitched voice? He had falsetto teeth.

"Alec," groaned his father when he saw his son's school report. "Why are you so awful at geography?"
"It's the teacher's fault, Dad. He keeps telling us about places I've never heard of."

Teacher: I was going to read you a story called *The Invasion of the Body Snatchers*, but I've changed my mind.
Class: Oh, why, Miss?
Teacher: Because we might get carried away.

"Mary," said her teacher, "you can't bring that lamb into school. What about the smell?"
"Oh, that's all right, Miss," said Mary. "It'll soon get used to it."

"That's an excellent essay for someone your age," said the English teacher.
"How about for someone my mum's age, Miss?"

Did you hear about the teacher whose pupils were such swots that when she walked into the classroom and said "Good morning", they wrote it in their notebooks?

"Well children," said the cannibal cookery teacher. "What did you make of the new English teacher?" "Burgers, Miss."

Mr Anderson, the absent-minded science teacher, brought a box into the classroom and said, "I've got a frog and a toad in here. When I get them out we'll look at the differences." He put his hand into the box and pulled out two sandwiches. "Oh, dear!" he said. "I could have sworn I'd just had my lunch."

When Dad came home he was astonished to see Alec sitting on a horse, writing something. "What on earth are you doing there?" he asked. "Well, teacher told us to write an essay on our favourite animal. That's why I'm here and that's why Susie's sitting in the goldfish bowl!"

The games teacher, Miss Janet Rockey,
Wanted to train as a jockey.
But, sad to recall,
She grew far too tall.
So now she teaches us hockey.

The night school teacher asked one of his pupils when he had last sat an exam.
"1945," said the chap.
"Good lord! That's more than 50 years ago."
"No, Sir! An hour and half, it's quarter past nine now."

"Welcome to school, Simon," said the nursery school teacher to the new boy. "How old are you?"
"I'm not old," said Simon. "I'm nearly new."

97

An English teacher asked her class to write an essay on what they'd do if they had £1,000,000. Alec handed in a blank sheet of paper.

"Alec!" yelled the teacher. "You've done nothing. Why?"

"Cos if I had £1,000,000 that's exactly what I would do."

Did you hear about the maths teacher who fainted in class?

Everyone tried to bring her 2.

Why did the maths teacher take a ruler to bed with him? He wanted to see how long he would sleep.

Typing teacher: Bob! Your work has certainly improved. There are only ten mistakes here.

Bob: Oh, good, Miss.

Teacher: Now let's look at the second line, shall we?

The headmaster was interviewing a new teacher. "You'll get £10,000 to start, with £15,000 after six months."
"Oh!" said the teacher. "I'll come back in six months then."

Why is a man wearing sunglasses like a rotten teacher?
Because he keeps his pupils in the dark.

Why are art galleries like retirement homes for teachers?
Because they're both full of old masters.

It was sweltering hot outside. The teacher came into the classroom wiping his brow and said, "Ninety-two today. Ninety-two."
"Happy birthday to you.
Happy birthday to you..."
sang the class.

The school teacher was furious when Alec knocked him down with his new bicycle in the playground. "Don't you know how to ride that thing?" he roared.
"Oh, yes!" shouted Alec over his shoulder. "It's the bell I can't work yet."

Why did the science teacher marry the school cleaner?
Because she swept him off his feet.

"I'm not going to school today," Alexander said to his mother. "The teachers bully me and the boys in my class don't like me."
"You're going. And that's final. I'll give you two good reasons why."
"Why?"
"Firstly, you're 35 years old. Secondly, you're the head teacher."

Please, Sir! Please, Sir! Why do you keep me locked up in this cage?
Because you're the teacher's pet.

Why did the teacher have her hair
in a bun?
Because she had her nose in a hamburger.

Joan's teacher wrote a letter of complaint to her
father. "What's all this about?" roared Dad. "Your
teacher says he finds it impossible to teach you
anything."

"I told you he was no good," said Joan.

Teacher: If you add 20,567 to 23,678 and then
divide by 97 what do you get?
Jim: The wrong answer.

Teacher: I see you don't cut your
hair any longer.
Nigel: No, Sir,
I cut it shorter.

Carol: Our teacher gives me the pip.
Darryl: What's her name?
Carol: Miss Lemmon.

Science Teacher: Can you tell me one substance that conducts electricity, Jane?
Jane: Why, er...
Science Teacher: That is correct.

Art Teacher: What colour would you paint the sun and the wind?
Brian: The sun rose, and the wind blue.

When is an English teacher like a judge?
When she hands out long sentences.

Teacher: Your books are a disgrace, Archibald. I don't see how anyone can possibly make as many mistakes in one day as you do.

Archibald: I get here early, Sir.

Teacher: Why do you want to work in a bank, Alan?

Alan: 'Cos there's money in it, Miss.

Biology Teacher: What kinds of birds do we get in captivity?

Janet: Jail birds, Miss!

Teacher: Who was that on the phone, Samantha?

Samantha: No one important, Miss. Just some man who said it was long-distance from Australia, so I told him I knew that already.

Teacher: You're wearing a very strange pair of socks, Darren. One's blue with red spots, and one's yellow with green stripes.

Darren: Yes, and I've got another pair just the same at home.

What do you call a teacher floating on a raft in the sea?
Bob.

Teacher: You weren't at school last Friday, Robert. I heard you were out playing football.

Robert: That's not true, Sir. And I've got the cinema tickets to prove it.

Teacher: What is the longest night of the year?
Alex: A fortnight.

Teacher: Recite your tables to me, Joan.

Joan: Dining-room table, kitchen table, bedside table...

Dave: Our teachers all do bird impressions.
Maeve: Really? What do they do?
Dave: They watch us like hawks.

Teacher: Martin, put some more water in the fish tank.
Martin: But, Sir, they haven't drunk the water I gave them yesterday.

Tracy: Would you punish someone for something they haven't done?
Teacher: Of course not.
Tracy: Oh, good, because I haven't done my homework.

Piano Tuner: I've come to tune the piano.
Music Teacher: But we didn't send for you.
Piano Tuner: No, but the people who live across the street did.

What does the music teacher do when he's locked out of the classroom?
Sing until he gets the right key.

Nigel: You said the school dentist would be painless, but he wasn't.
Teacher: Did he hurt you?
Nigel: No, but he screamed when I bit his finger.

Teacher: And why would you like to be a teacher, Clarence?
Clarence: Because I wouldn't have to learn anything, Sir. I'd know everything by then.

Teacher: Name six things that contain milk.
    Daft Dora: Custard, cocoa, and four cows.

A teacher took her class for a walk
in the country, and Susie found a
grass snake. "Come quickly, Miss,"
she called, "here's a tail without
a body!"

Music Student: Did you really learn to play
              the violin in six easy lessons?
    Music Teacher: Yes, but the 500 that
              followed were pretty difficult.

Teacher: Didn't you
know the bell
had gone?
Silly Sue: I didn't
take it, Miss.

Teacher: Who can tell me what an archaeologist is?

Tracey: It's someone whose career is in ruins.

Teacher: Barbara, name three collective nouns.

Barbara: The wastepaper basket, the dustbin and the vacuum cleaner.

Teacher: Who knows what a hippy is?

Clever Dick: It's something that holds your leggy on.

Teacher: Can anyone tell me what a shamrock is?

Jimmy: It's a fake diamond, Miss.

Caspar: I was the teacher's pet last
year.
Jasper: Why was that?
Caspar: She couldn't afford a dog.

Teacher: Who can tell me
where Turkey is?
Dumb Donald: We ate ours
last Christmas, Miss.

Teacher: Why are you always late?
Roger: I threw away my alarm clock.
Teacher: But why did you throw away your alarm
clock?
Roger: Because it always went off when I was
asleep.

Geography
teacher: What is
the coldest place
in the world?
Ann: Chile.

Barbara: I wish I'd been alive a few hundred years ago.
History teacher: Why?
Barbara: There'd have been a lot less history to learn.

Teacher: Write "I must not forget my gym kit" 100 times.
Nicky: But, Sir, I only forgot it once.

English Teacher: Now give me a sentence using the word "fascinate".
Clara: My raincoat has ten buttons but I can only fasten eight.

Teacher: Why do birds fly south in winter?
Jim: Because it's too far to walk.

SOUTH

Teacher: Colin, one of your essays is very good, but the other one I can't read.

Colin: Yes, Sir. My mother is a much better writer than my father.

Teacher: What happened to your homework?
Boy: I made it into a paper plane and someone hijacked it.

Teacher: Why are you standing on your head?
Boy: I'm just trying to turn things over in my mind, Sir.

Teacher: Who can tell me what "BC" stands for?
Girl: Before calculators?

A little boy came home from his first day at school and said to his mother, "What's the use of going to school? I can't read, I can't write and the teacher won't let me talk."

Teacher: Were you copying his sums?
Girl: No, Sir. I was just looking to see if he'd got his right.

Teacher: In this exam you will be allowed ten minutes for each question.
Boy: How long is the answer?

Teacher: Billy, didn't you hear me call you?
Billy: Yes, Miss, but you told us yesterday not to answer back.

Teacher: I wish you'd pay a little attention.
Girl: I'm paying as little as possible.

Teacher: If I had ten flies on my desk, and I swatted one, how many flies would be left?
Girl: One — the dead one!

Teacher: What is the outer part of a tree called?
Sam: Don't know, Sir.
Teacher: Bark, boy, bark!
Sam: Woof! Woof!

"Frank," said the weary maths teacher, "if you had seven pounds in one pocket, and seven pounds in another pocket, what would you have?"
"Someone else's trousers!"

"Melanie," said the teacher sharply, "you've been doing Rebecca's homework for her again! I recognized your writing in her exercise book."
"I haven't, Miss," declared Melanie. "It's just that we use the same pencil!"

"Philip," asked the chemistry teacher, "what is HNO3?"
"Oh, er... just a minute, Miss, er... it's on the tip of my tongue..."
"Well, in that case — spit it out. It's nitric acid!"

"Any complaints?" asked the teacher during school dinner.
"Yes, sir," said one bold lad, "these peas are awfully hard, sir."
The master dipped a spoon into the peas on the boy's plate and tasted them.
"They seem soft enough to me," he declared.
"Yes, they are now, I've been chewing them for the last half hour."

Teacher: Martin, I've taught you everything I know, and you're still ignorant!

Teacher: Tommy Russell, you're late again.
Tommy: Sorry, sir. It's my bus — it's always coming late.
Teacher: Well, if it's late again tomorrow, catch an earlier one.

Teacher: Alan, give me a sentence starting with "I".
Alan: "I" is-
Teacher: No, Alan. You must always say "I am".
Alan: Oh, right. "I" am the ninth letter of the alphabet.

Teacher: Ford, you're late for school again. What is it this time?
Ford: I sprained my ankle, sir.
Teacher: That's a lame excuse.

Teacher: Carol, what is "can't" short for?
Carol: Cannot.
Teacher: And what is "don't" short for?
Carol: Doughnut!

Teacher: Anyone here quick at picking up music?
Terence and Tony: I am, sir!
Teacher: Right, you two. Move that piano!

Teacher: How do you spell
"gooseberry"?
Pupil: G-u-z-b-r-y.
Teacher: The dictionary spells it
g-o-o-s-e-b-e-r-r-y.
Pupil: You didn't ask me how
the dictionary spells it!

Teacher: If I had 40 gooseberries in one hand and 40 in the other, what would I have?
Pupil: Big hands.

Dave: What did your teacher say when you took your pet bulldog to school?
Don: He said, "You can't bring that ugly brute in here."
Dave: What happened then?
Don: The bulldog said, "It's not my fault, he brought me."

Teacher? If I cut two bananas and two apples into ten pieces each, what will I get?
Pupil: A fruit salad.

The teacher was trying to instil into her class the virtues of hard work. "Take," she said, "the example of the ant. It works and works all the time. And what is the result of all this work?"

Clever Clogs Charlie: "Someone treads on it, Miss."

Teacher: What's the difference between the death rate in Elizabethan times and the death rate nowadays?

Smart Sue: It's the same, Miss - one death per person.

Paddy: Would you say the kids at your school are tough?

Maddie: Tough? Even the teachers play truant!

Animal Crackers

What is a hen's favourite TV programme?
The Eggs Files.

What's pink, curly and cuts the grass?
A prawn-mower.

What goes "Rivet. Help! Rivet. Help!"?
A frog with a man in his throat.

What do you get if you cross
Rudolph with a weatherman?
Rain, dear.

Which tigers live in old trees?
Cat-a-logs.

What do cows read?
Moospapers.

If dolphins are so intelligent, why do they live in schools?

What's the best way to cook an ape?
Butter it and put it under the gorilla.

Did you cook me some spaghetti?
– No.
Then I'm afraid I just ate your wormery.

What do you get if you cross a
worm with a young goat?
A dirty kid.

What do you get if you cross a
snake with a pig?
A boar constrictor.

What's the difference between
a fly and a bird?
A bird can fly but a fly can't bird.

Why did the sparrow fly into the library?
It was looking for bookworms.

What do you call a snake that is trying to become a bird?
A feather boa.

What do two lovesick owls say when it's raining?
Too-wet-to-woo!

What sits in a tree and says "Hoots mon, hoots mon"?
A Scottish owl.

Why were the mummy and daddy owls worried about their son?
Because he didn't seem to give a hoot any more.

What does an educated owl say?
Whom.

Why did the owl, 'owl?
Because the woodpecker would peck 'er.

What do confused owls say?
Too-whit-to-why?

What did the owl say to his friend as he flew off?
Owl be seeing you later.

"I told you to draw a picture of a cow eating grass," said the art master. "Why have you handed in a blank sheet of paper?"
"Because the cow ate all the grass, that's why there's no grass."
"But what about the cow?"
"There wasn't much point in it hanging around when there was nothing to eat, so it went back to the cow shed."

What did the baby owl's parents say when he wanted to go to a party? "You're not owld enough."

What did the owls do when one of them had a punk haircut? They hooted with laughter.

**What do Scottish owls sing?
"Owld Lang Syne."**

**What did the scornful owl say?
"Twit twoo."**

**How do you know that owls are
cleverer than chickens?
Have you ever heard of Kentucky
Fried Owl?**

**What do you get if you cross King
Kong with a budgie?
A messy cage.**

What do you get if you cross an owl with a witch?
A bird that's ugly but doesn't give a hoot.

What does a headless horseman ride?
A nightmare.

Which bird is always out of breath?
A puffin.

What's the difference between a gymnastics teacher and a duck?
One goes quick on its legs, the other goes quack on its legs.

Donald: My canary died of 'flu.
Dora: I didn't know canaries got 'flu.
Donald: Mine flew into a car.

An idiot decided to start a chicken farm so he bought a hundred chickens to start. A month later he returned to the dealer for another hundred chickens because all of the first lot had died. A month later he was back at the dealers for another hundred chickens, for the second lot had also died. "But I think I know where I'm going wrong," said the idiot. "I think I'm planting them too deep."

My sister is so dumb, she thinks that a buttress is a female goat.

Did you hear about the idiot who made his chickens drink boiling water?
He thought they would lay hard-boiled eggs.

What happened when the cows got out of their field?
There was udder chaos.

Two owls were playing pool.
One said "Two hits."
The other replied "Two hits to who?"

Why did the vulture
cross the road?
For a fowl reason.

Why don't
vultures fly
south in the
winter?
Because they
can't afford
the air fare.

Why did a man's pet vulture not make a sound for five years?
It was stuffed.

What do you call a team of vultures playing football?
Fowl play.

What's a vulture's favourite soap opera?
Coronation Tweet.

Why should a school not be near a chicken farm?
To avoid the pupils overhearing fowl language.

Mary had a bionic cow,
It lived on safety pins.
And every time she milked
that cow,
The milk came out in tins.

On which side does a
chicken have the most
feathers?
On the outside.

What did the
neurotic pig say to
the farmer?
You take me for
grunted.

How do hens
dance?
Chick to chick.

What do you give a sick pig? Oinkment.

A woodpecker was pecking a hole in a tree. All of a sudden a flash of lightning struck the tree to the ground. The woodpecker looked bemused for a moment and then said: "Gee, I guess I don't know my own strength."

Who led 10,000 pigs up a hill and back again? The Grand Old Duke of Pork.

A monster decided to become a TV
star, so he went to see an agent.
"What do you do?" asked the agent.
"Bird impressions," said the
monster.
"What kind of bird impressions?"
"I eat worms."

What do you call a pig thief?
A hamburglar.

Where do rich pigs live in America?
In a sty scraper.

Why is a leg of pork like
an old radio?
Because both of
them have lots
of crackling.

What happened to the pig who studied Shakespeare?
He ended up in Hamlet.

Why should you never tell a secret to a pig?
Because they're all squealers.

What's pink and wobbly and plays football?
Queens Pork Rangers.

Why didn't the piglets listen to their grandfather?
Because he was an old boar.

What did one pig say to the other?
"Let's be pen pals."

This morning a chicken jumped off a bridge into a river. Police think it was fed up with jokes about crossing the road.

How do you know you are haunted by a parrot?
He keeps saying "Oooo's a pretty boy then?"

How do you count cows?
With a cowculator!

What do you get if you cross a hen with some gunpowder?
An eggsplosion.

What do you get if you cross a nun and a chicken?
A pecking order.

Would you like a duck egg for tea?
Only if you "quack" it for me.

My budgie lays square eggs.
That's amazing! Can it talk as well?
Yes, but only one word.
What's that?
Ouch!

What is a bird's favourite computer game?
Tweet Fighter.

What do you get if you cross a centipede with a parrot?
A walkie-talkie.

Margarine is a fat made from imitation cows.

I wish I were a
little bird
Hiding in a
tree.
Then when
you passed
along below
I'd spatter you
with me.

Where do vultures meet for coffee?
In a nest-café.

What's a crow's favourite television programme? Rookside.

Where do the toughest vultures come from? Hard-boiled eggs.

What do you call a woodpecker with no beak? A head-banger.

Why couldn't the vulture talk to the dove? Because he didn't speak pigeon English.

What do a vulture, a pelican and a taxman have in common? Big bills!

How do we know vultures are religious? Because they're birds of prey.

What do you get if you cross a parrot with a soldier?
A Parrot trooper.

Did you hear about the scientist who crossed a parrot with a crocodile?
It bit off his arm and said, "Who's a pretty boy then?"

Did you hear about the man who brought his mother a very rare parrot for her birthday? It could speak ten languages, play chess and sing the entire works of Mozart. He asked her what she thought of the bird. "It was delicious son," she said, "absolutely delicious..."

Knock, Knock.
Who's there?
Scott.
Scott who?
Scott nothing to
do with you!

Knock, Knock.
Who's there?
Omelette.
Omelette who?
Omelette
smarter
than I look!

Knock, knock. Who's there? Sacha. Sacha who? Sacha lot of questions on this exam!

Knock, knock.
Who's there?
Pecan.
Pecan who?
Pecan somebody
your own size.

Knock, knock.
Who's there?
Fanny.
Fanny who?
Fanny the way you keep
saying "Who's there?"
every time I knock!

Knock, Knock.
Who's there?
Ooze.
Ooze who?
Ooze that
knocking
at my door?

Knock, knock.
Who's there?
Colleen.
Colleen who?
Colleen yourself up,
you look filthy.

Knock, Knock.
Who's there?
Anita Loos.
Anita Loos who?
Anita Loos
about 20
pounds.

Knock, knock.
Who's there?
Eel.
Eel who?
Eel meet again.

Knock, knock.
Who's there?
Yule.
Yule who?
Yule never know
just how much I
love you.

Knock, knock.
Who's there?
Russia.
Russia who?
Russiaway from
this place - quick!

Knock,
knock.
Who's there?
Teacher.
Teacher
who?
Teacher-self
French.

Knock,
knock.
Who's
there?
Canoe.
Canoe who?
Canoe help
me with my
homework,
please,
Dad, I'm
stuck.

Knock, knock.
Who's there?
Francis.
Francis who?
Francis a
country in
Europe.

145

Knock, knock. Who's there? Bella. Bella who? Bella not working, that's why I knocka.

Knock, knock. Who's there? Quiet Tina. Quiet Tina who? Quiet Tina classroom.

Knock, knock. Who's there? Noah. Noah who? Noah good place to eat?

Knock, knock. Who's there? Alison. Alison who? Alison to my teacher!

Knock, knock.
Who's there?
Ida.
Ida who?
Ida nawful
time at school
today.

Knock, knock.
Who's there?
Genoa.
Genoa who?
Genoa good
teacher?

Will you remember me in one day's time?
Of course I will.
Will you remember me in a week's time?
Of course I will.
Will you remember me in a year's time?
Of course I will.
Will you remember me in ten years' time?
Of course I will.
Knock, knock.
Who's there?
See, you've forgotten
me already!

Knock, knock.
Who's there?
Olive.
Olive who?
Olive across the
road.

**Knock, knock.
Who's there?
Sonia.
Sonia who?
Sonia shoe, I can
smell it from here.**

**Knock, knock.
Who's there?
Little old lady.
Little old lady
who?
I didn't know you
could yodel**

Knock, knock.
Who's there?
Thumping.
Thumping who?
Thumping green
and slimy just
went up your
trousers.

Knock, knock.
Who's there?
Olga.
Olga who?
Olga home if you're
horrid to me again.

Knock, Knock.
Who's there?
Turnip.
Turnip who?
Turnip for work at
nine or you're
fired!

Knock,
knock.
Who's
there?
Dishes.
Dishes
who?
Dishes
the way
I talk
now I've
got
falsh
teeth.

149

Knock, Knock.
Who's there?
Cook.
Cook who?
Cuckoo yourself! I
didn't come here
to be insulted.

Knock, knock.
Who's there?
Tuna.
Tuna who?
Tuna violin and it
will sound better!

Knock, knock.
Who's there?
Watson.
Watson who?
Watson the menu
today?

Knock, knock.
Who's there?
Egbert.
Egbert who?
Egbert no
bacon.

Knock, knock.
Who's there?
Victor.
Victor who?
Victor his football shorts.

Knock, knock.
Who's there?
Dozen.
Dozen who?
Dozen anyone know how to play?

Knock, knock.
Who's there?
Stopwatch.
Stopwatch who?
Stopwatch you're doing this minute!

Knock, knock.
Who's there?
Honda.
Honda who?
Honda stand what
I'm talking about?

Knock, knock.
Who's there?
Datsun.
Datsun who?
Datsun other
lousy joke!

Knock, knock.
Who's there?
Stan.
Stan who?
Stan back, his
breath smells
awful!

**Knock,
knock.
Who's there?
Juliet.
Juliet who?
Juliet so
much she
burst!**

Knock,
knock.
Who's there?
Datsun.
Datsun who?
Datsun awful
dress you're
wearing!

Knock, knock.
Who's there.
Joan.
Joan who?
Joan call us,
we'll call you!

Knock,
knock.
Who's
there?
Flea.
Flea
who?
Flea's a
jolly
good
fellow.

Knock, knock.
Who's there?
Tom Sawyer.
Tom Sawyer
who?
Tom Sawyer
bum when
you were
changing
your
trousers.

Knock,
knock.
Who's there?
Weevil.
Weevil who?
Weevil work
it out.

Knock, knock.
Who's there?
Flea.
Flea who?
Flea thirty in
the afternoon.

Knock, knock.
Who's there?
Webster.
Webster who?
Webster Spin,
your friendly
neighbourhood
spider.

Knock, knock.
Who's there?
Moth.
Moth who?
Motht people
know the
anthwer.

**Knock,
knock.
Who's
there?
Earwig.
Earwig
who?
Earwig
come!**

154

Knock, knock.
Who's there?
Grub.
Grub who?
Grub hold of my
hand and let's go!

Knock, knock.
Who's there?
Roach.
Roach who?
Roach out and
touch somebody.

Knock, knock.
Who's there?
Larva.
Larva who?
Larva cup
of coffee.

Knock, knock.
Who's there?
Bee.
Bee who?
Bee careful out
there!

Knock, knock.
Who's there?
Army Ants.
Army Ants who?
Army Ants coming
for tea then?

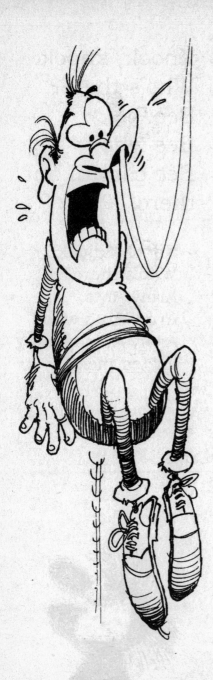

Knock, knock.
Who's there?
Amos.
Amos who?
A mosquito.

**Knock, knock.
Who's there?
Anna.
Anna who?
Anna 'nother
mosquito.**

Knock, knock.
Who's there?
Insect.
Insect who?
Insect your name
and address here.

**Knock knock.
Who's there?
Tristan.
Tristan who?
Tristan insect to
get right up your
nose!**

Banana Skins

What is an orange's favourite TV show?
Top of the Pips.

Which fruit is a TV star?
The Nickberry.

How do oranges play cricket?
They use fruit bats.

Boy: These peaches are really tough to eat.
Girl: They're tinned.

What do you call a fruit that plays the guitar and sings harmony?
John Lemmon.

An orange and a plum had a
race. Who won?
The plum. The orange was
pipped at the post.

What do you get if
you cross a juicy
fruit with a sad dog?
A melon collie.

What is the best fruit
for children?
An Opear.

What do hairy
fruit shave with?
Raisin blades.

What's the longest film
ever made?
James and the Giant
Speech.

What's the fruitiest film ever made? Planet of the Apricots.

Which type of fruit landed on the moon? Apple O-Eleven.

Where did the mango? He plum disappeared!

Why did Adam and Eve start wearing clothes? Cos Figs Ain't Wot They Use to Be.

What are the best
things to put in a
fruit cake?
Teeth!

What do vampire footballers have at
half-time?
Blood oranges.

What do you get if you cross an
orange with a comedian?
Peels of laughter.

Why did the orange
go to the doctor?
Because it wasn't
peeling well.

Why couldn't the orange get up the hill?
Because it had run out of juice.

What do you get if you cross a plum with a man-eating monster?
A purple people-eater.

"What kind of pie do you call this?" asked one school-boy indignantly.
"What's it taste of?" asked the cook.
"Glue!"
"Then it's apple pie — the plum pie tastes of soap."

What's purple and hums?
A rotten plum!

What do you call an overweight pumpkin?
A plumpkin.

Why is plum pudding like the
sea?
Because it is full of currants.

When is plum pudding musical?
When it is piping hot.

Teacher: If you saw me standing by a witch,
what fruit would it remind you of?
Pupil: A pear.

What was Noah's occupation?
Preserving pears.

Harry: Please may I
have another pear,
Miss?
Teacher: Another,
Harry? They
don't grow
on trees,
you know.

Why are monsters big and hairy? So that you can tell them apart from gooseberries.

Teacher: Who can tell me what geese eat? Paul: Er, gooseberries, Sir?

My mother uses lemon juice for her complexion. Maybe that is why she always looks so sour.

"Can I have another slice of lemon?" a man in a pub asked the barmaid.
"We don't have any lemons in this pub!"
"Oh, no!" said the man. "If that's true, I've just squeezed your canary into my gin and tonic!"

What do you do with a
hurt lemon?
Give it lemon-aid.

What do you get if cross a bottle of
lemonade with a masseur?
A fizzy o'therapist.

What did the elephant say to
the lemon?
Let's play squash.

Did you ever see a lemon peel or
a banana peel?
No, but I once saw an
apple turnover.

Samantha: Do you really love me?

Simon: Oh yes.

Samantha: Then whisper something soft and sweet in my ear.

Simon: Lemon meringue pie.

What's big, purple and lies in the sea?
Grape Britain.

What's purple
and burns?
The Grape Fire
of London.

What's purple and
4,000 miles long?
The Grape Wall of China.

What did the grape say when
the elephant trod on it?
Nothing – it just gave a little
wine.

What's purple and barks at people?
A grape dane.

Who swings
through the
Vines?
Tarzan of
the Grapes.

Why don't grapefruit tie
their own shoelaces?
If you were shaped like a
grapefruit, you couldn't see
your feet either.

How did the baker get an
electric shock?
He stood on a bun
and a currant
ran up his leg.

What's purple and wobbles in the corner of your living room? Blackcurrant jelly-vision.

"Those currant buns you sold me yesterday had three cockroaches in them," a woman complained over the phone to a baker. "Sorry about that," said the baker. "If you bring the cockroaches back I'll give you the three currants I owe you."

A man saw a gardener pushing a wheelbarrow full of manure. "Where are you going with that?" he asked. "Going to put it on my blackcurrants," said the gardener. "Suit yourself," said the man. "I usually put sugar and cream on mine."

Why did the raspberry jelly wobble?
Because it saw the strawberry milk-
shake.

What do you have when 2,000 strawber-
ries try to get through a door together?
Strawberry Jam.

How can you tell when there is an elephant
in your strawberry blancmange?
It's especially lumpy.

What do you call a two-tonne
strawberry with a nasty temper?
Sir!

What's red and dangerous?
Raspberry
and
tarantula
jelly.

Time flies like an arrow, but fruit flies like a banana.

What's red and goes at 60 mph? A strawberry on a motorbike.

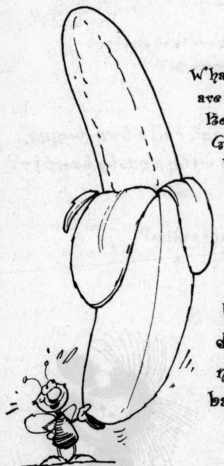

What should you do if you are on a picnic with King Kong?
Give him the biggest bananas.

How do you catch King Kong?
Hang upside down and make a noise like a banana.

Why did the wizard wear a yellow robe to the Halloween party?
He was going as a banana.

Tom: What did the banana say to the elephant?
Nik: I don't know.
Tom: Nothing. Bananas can't talk.

What's yellow and flashes?
A banana with a loose connection.

1st witch: Here's a banana if you can spell it.
2nd witch: I can spell banana. I just don't know when to stop.

Mandy: Our teacher went on a special banana diet.
Andy: Did she lose weight?
Mandy: No, but she couldn't half climb trees well!

What's the easiest way to make a banana split?
Cut it in half.

What is yellow and goes click-click?
A ballpoint banana.

Why didn't the banana snore?
'Cos it was afraid to wake up the rest of the bunch.

What's yellow and has 22 legs?
Banana United.

What did the handsome boy banana say to the pretty girl banana?
"You appeal to me."

What's yellow on the inside and green on the outside?
A banana disguised as a cucumber.

What is the hardest thing to eat?
A banana sideways.

What do you call a gorilla with two bananas in his ears? Anything you like, because he can't hear you.

A woman with a baby in her arms was sitting in a station waiting room, sobbing miserably. A porter came up to her and asked her what the problem was. "Some people were in here just now and they were so rude about my little boy," she cried. "They all said he was ugly." "There, there, don't cry" said the porter kindly. "Shall I get you a nice cup of tea?" "Thank you, that would be nice," replied the woman, wiping her eyes. "You're very kind." "That's all right. Don't mention it," said the porter. "While I'm at it, would you like a banana for your gorilla?"

Jenny: I've heard they're not going to grow bananas in Jamaica any longer.
Kenny: Why not?
Jenny: They're long enough already!

Why are bullies like bananas?
Because they're yellow and hang around in bunches.

James: I call my girlfriend "Peach".
John: Because she's beautiful?
James: No, because she's got a heart of stone!

First boy: She had a beautiful pair of eyes, her skin had the glow of a peach, her cheeks were like apples and her lips like cherries - that's my girl.
Second boy: Sounds like a fruit salad to me.

What's a good way of putting on weight?
Eat a peach, swallow the centre, and you've gained a stone.

Your cheeks are like peaches – football peetches.

Why is history like a fruit cake?
Because it's full of dates.

Why did the strawberry go out with the prune?
Because it couldn't find a date.

A cobra was invited to dine
By his charmingly cute valentine.
But when he got there
He found that the fare
Was pineapple dumplings with wine.

What do you get if you cross an apple with a Christmas tree?
A pine-apple.

Why didn't the two worms go into Noah's Ark in an apple?
Because everyone had to go in pairs.

What did one maggot say to the other who was stuck in an apple?
"Worm your way out of that one, then!"

What's worse than finding a maggot in your apple?
Finding half a maggot in your apple.

What's the maggot army called? The apple corps.

What lives in apples and is an avid reader? A bookworm.

1st apple: You look down in the dumps. What's eating you?
2nd apple: Worms, I think.

What do you get if you cross an apple with a shellfish? A crab apple.

Teacher: Who was the
first woman on earth?
Angela: I don't know, Sir.
Teacher: Come on, Angela,
it has something to do
with an apple.
Angela: Granny Smith?

Trevor came rushing in to his Dad.
"Dad," he puffed, "is it true that an
apple a day keeps the doctor away?"
"That's what they say," said his Dad.
"Well, give us an apple quick — I've
just broken the
doctor's window!"

Damien was being severely ticked off by his father for fighting. "Now, Damien," said his angry parent, "this will not do! You must learn that you can't have everything you want in this life. There must always be give and take." "But there was, Dad!" protested the aggressive youngster. "I gave him a black eye and took the apple."

When an apple hits a banana, what is it called? A fruit punch.

What are you doing in my apple tree, young man? One of your apples fell down, sir, and I'm putting it back.

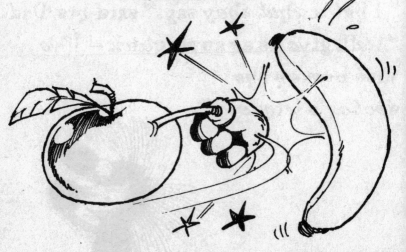

Large as Life

GAA GAA— GOO GOO—

What do you call an elephant
with a TV in its stomach?
An Eletubby.

What do you call a
dream about
elephants?
An elephantasy.

Why did the elephant put on armour?
Because he was into heavy metal.

What do you call an
elephant with a fat
tummy?
A Bellyphant.

**Where do elephants shop?
At the jumbo sale.**

**Where do elephants go on holiday?
Tuskany.**

AAAARRRGG

**What did the Speak-Your-Weight machine say to the elephant?
Aaaaaaaaaarrrrrrrrggggggghhhhh!**

**What do you get if you mix an elephant with a strawberry?
Jambo.**

**What do you get if you cross an
elephant with some locusts?
I'm not sure, but if they ever swarm -
watch out!**

**What do you get if you cross a
worm with an elephant?
Big holes in your garden.**

**What do you get if you cross a mouse
with an elephant?
Big holes in your skirting boards.**

**How can you prevent an elephant
from charging?
Take away his credit card.**

Boy: What's the biggest ant in the world?
Girl: My aunt Fatima.
Boy: No, it's an elephant.
Girl: You obviously haven't met my aunt Fatima.

What is Smokey the Elephant's middle name?
The.

What do you get if you cross an elephant with a spider?
I don't know, but if it crawled over your ceiling the house would collapse.

What do you get if you cross an elephant with the abominable snowman?
A jumbo yeti.

A cannibal was walking through the jungle when he came to a clearing and saw a freshly-killed elephant lying down with a pigmy standing on top of it, brandishing a big stick and doing a victory dance. "Have you just killed that elephant?" asked the cannibal. "Yes," replied the pigmy, "I did it with my club."

"Wow," said the cannibal, "you must have a really big club!"

"Yes," replied the pigmy, "there are about 40 of us in it!"

"Why are you tearing up your homework notebook and scattering the pieces around the playground?" a furious teacher asked one of her pupils.

"To keep the elephants away, Miss."

"There are no elephants."

"Shows how effective it is then, doesn't it?"

"Please, Miss!" said a little boy at kindergarten. "We're going to play elephants and circuses, do you want to join in?" "I'd love to," said the teacher. "What do you want me to do?" "You can be the lady that feeds us peanuts!"

Which animals were the last to leave Noah's Ark? The elephants – they were packing their trunks.

What's the best thing to give a seasick elephant? Plenty of room.

Why did the elephant paint her head yellow? To see if blondes really do have more fun.

Anna: I was top of the class last week.
Mum: How did you manage that?
Anna: I managed to answer a question about elephants.
Mum: What question?
Anna: Well, the teacher asked us how many legs an elephant had, and I said five.
Mum: But that wasn't right.
Anna: I know, but it was the nearest anyone got.

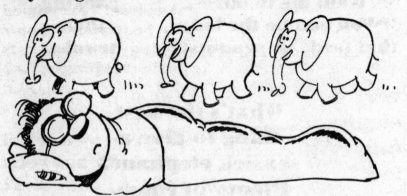

My dad is so short-sighted he can't get to sleep unless he counts elephants.

Did you hear about the ogre who threw trunks over cliffs? Nothing special about that, you might think – but the elephants were still attached.

What do you get if you cross an elephant and peanut butter? An elephant that sticks to the roof of your mouth.

How does an elephant go up a tree?
It sits on an acorn and waits for it to grow.

Why do elephants have flat feet?
From jumping out of tall trees.

A Scotsman paying his first visit to the zoo stopped by one of the cages. "An' whut animal would that be?" he asked the keeper.
"That's a moose from Canada," came the reply.
"A moose!" exclaimed the Scotsman. "Hoots – they must ha' rats like elephants over there."

How can you tell if an elephant has been sleeping in your bed?
The sheets are wrinkled and the bed smells of peanuts.

189

Is the squirt from an elephant's trunk very powerful?
Of course – a jumbo jet can keep 500 people in the air for hours at a time.

How do you make an elephant sandwich?
First of all you get a very large loaf...

What is the difference between a gooseberry and an elephant?
Pick them up - an elephant is usually heavier.

If you cross an elephant with a goldfish, would you get swimming trunks?

Remember: when eating an elephant, take one bite at a time.

Elephants are modest - they bathe with their trunks.

How do elephants climb down from trees? They sit on a leaf and wait 'til fall.

How can you tell if there are elephants in your refrigerator? Footprints in the cream cheese.

Why do elephants have trunks? Because they don't have glove compartments.

How do you know peanuts are fattening? Have you ever seen a skinny elephant?

How many elephants can you get into a mini? Two in the front and two in the back.

How many rhinoceroses can you get in a mini? Four, take the elephants out first.

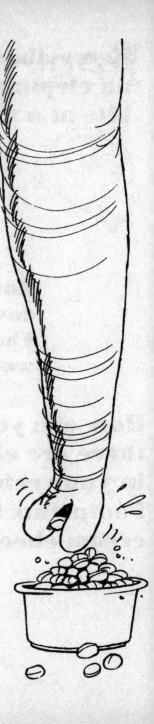

Pesky Pets

What do angry rodents send
each other at Christmas?
Cross mouse cards.

Which mouse was a Roman emperor?
Julius Cheeser.

Hickory dickory dock
The mice ran up the clock.
The clock struck one,
And the rest got away with minor injuries.

What is grey and hairy and lives on a man's face?
A mousetache.

What do you call a mouse that can
pick up a monster?
Sir.

How do mice celebrate when they move house?
With a mouse-warming party.

What did the mouse say when his friend broke his front teeth?
Hard cheese.

Why did the mouse eat a candle?
For light refreshment.

What is a mouse's favourite game?
Hide and squeak.

What goes "dot, dot, dash, squeak"?
Mouse code.

What do you get if
you cross a mouse
with a packet of
soap powder?
Bubble and Squeak.

Who has large antlers,
has a high voice and
wears white gloves?
Mickey Moose.

Why do mice need
oiling?
Because they
squeak.

What is a mouse's
favourite record?
Please cheese me.

What's a rat's least
favourite record?
What's up, Pussycat.

How do you save a drowning rodent? Use mouse to mouse resuscitation.

What kind of musical instrument do rats play? Mouse organ.

How can you tell the difference between a rabbit and a red-eyed monster? Just try getting a red-eyed monster into a rabbit hutch.

Why was the Abominable Snowman's dog called Frost? Because Frost bites.

What has six legs and flies? A witch giving her cat a lift.

Why are black cats such good singers?
They're very mewsical.

When it is unlucky to see a black cat?
When you're a mouse.

What do you call it when a witch's cat falls off her broomstick?
A catastrophe.

What do you get if you cross a witch's cat with Father Christmas?
Santa Claws.

How do you get milk from a witch's cat?
Steal her saucer.

What do cats like for breakfast?
Mice Krispies.

What is an octopus?
An eight-sided cat.

Why do black cats never shave?
Because eight out of ten cats prefer
Whiskas.

What did the black cat say to the
fish head?
I've got a bone to pick with you.

What do you get if you cross a
jellyfish with a sheepdog?
Colliewobbles.

What do you call a cat who never comes when she's called?
Im-puss-able.

What's furry, has whiskers and chases outlaws?
A posse cat.

Now you see it . . . now you don't - what are you looking at?
A black cat walking over a zebra crossing.

What has four legs, a tail, whiskers and cuts grass?
A lawn miaower.

What do you get if you cross a cat and a duck?
A duck-filled fatty puss.

What do you call a witch's cat who can spring from the ground to her mistress's hat in one leap?
A good jum-purr.

What do witches' cats strive for?
Purr-fection.

What do you call a witch's cat who can do spells as well as her mistress?
An ex-purr-t.

Why did the skeleton run up a tree?
Because a dog was after its bones.

First cat: Where do fleas go in winter?
Second cat: Search me!

What did Dr Frankenstein get when he put his goldfish's brain in the body of his dog?
I don't know, but it's great at chasing submarines.

There once was a very strong cat
Who had a fight with a bat.
The bat flew away
And at the end of the day
The cat had a scrap with a rat.

Mother: Keep that dog out of the house, it's full of fleas.
Son: Keep out of the house, Fido, it's full of fleas.

Wizard: Have you put the cat out?
Witch: Why? Was he burning?

Why is a frog luckier than a cat?
Because a frog croaks all the time - a cat only croaks nine times.

Emm: What's the name of your dog?
Nik: Ginger.
Emm: Does Ginger bite?
Nik: No, but Ginger snaps.

What did the clean dog say to the insect?
Long time no flea!

What's the difference between fleas and dogs?
Dogs can have fleas, but fleas can't have dogs.

What's the difference between a flea-bitten dog and a bored visitor?
One's going to itch. The other's itching to go.

"Leave me alone, just let me live one of my own lives," said the young cat to its parents.

Why was the mother flea feeling down in the dumps?
Because she thought her children were all going to the dogs.

A wizard went to the doctor one day complaining of headaches. "It's because I live in the same room as two of my brothers," he said. "One of them has six goats and the other has four pigs and they all live in the room with us. The smell is terrible."

"Well couldn't you just open the windows?" asked the doctor.

"Certainly not," he replied, "my bats would fly out."

What happened to the skeleton that was attacked by a dog?
It ran off with some bones and left him without a leg to stand on.

What did one black cat say to the other?
Nothing. Cats can't speak.

What did the black cat do when its tail was cut off?
It went to a re-tail store.

It's obvious that animals are smarter than humans. Put eight horses in a race and 20,000 people will go along to see it. But put eight people in a race and not one horse will bother to go along and watch.

Jim: Our dog is just like one of the family.
Fred: Which one?

There was once a puppy called May who loved to pick quarrels with animals who were bigger than she was. One day she argued with a lion. The next day was the first of June.
Why?
Because that was the end of May!

What kind of cats love water?
Octopusses.

My dog saw a sign that said "Wet Paint" - so he did!

My dog is a nuisance. He chases everyone on a bicycle. What can I do? Take his bike away.

A man went into the local department store where he saw a sign on the escalator - "Dogs must be carried on this escalator". The man then spent the next two hours looking for a dog.

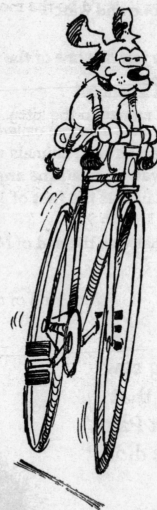

What's a twip?
What a wabbit calls a twain wide!

"I'm sorry to call you out at this time of night," said the witch, "but it's my poor black cat. He's just lying there telling me he wants to die." The monster vet licked his lips. "Well, you've done the right thing by sending for me..."

A motorist approached the Headmaster one afternoon and said, "I'm awfully sorry, but I think I've just run over the school cat. Can I replace it?" The Headmaster looked him up and down and replied, "I doubt if you'd be the mouser she was."

What happened when the cat
swallowed a penny?
There was money in the kitty.

What do ghosts like about
riding horses?
Ghoulloping.

Did you hear about the witch who fed her pet
vulture on sawdust?
The vulture laid ten eggs and when
they hatched, nine chicks had wooden
legs and the tenth
was a woodpecker.

What fish do dogs chase?
Catfish.

What pet makes the loudest noise?
A trum-pet.

What dog smells of onions?
A hot dog.

I'd like to buy
a dog.
Certainly, sir. Any
particular breed? A red
setter, perhaps?
No, not a
red setter.
A golden Labrador?
No, not a golden
Labrador. I don't want a
coloured dog, just a
black-and-white one.
Why a black-and-white
one, sir?
Isn't the licence
cheaper?

My dog plays chess.
Your dog plays chess?
He must be really
clever!
Oh, I don't know.
I usually beat him
three times out
of four.

**So you are distantly
related to the family
next door, are you ?
Yes - their dog is our
dog's brother.**

This loaf is nice and warm!
It should be - the cat's been sitting on it all day!

Would you like to play with our new dog?
He looks very fierce. Does he bite?
That's what I want to find out.

What's your new dog's name?
Dunno - he won't tell me.

Sign in shop window: FOR
SALE Pedigree bulldog.
House-trained. Eats anything.
Very fond of children.

A man who bought a dog
took it back, complaining
that it made a mess all
over the house. "I thought
you said it was house-
trained," he moaned.
"So it is," said the
previous owner. "It won't
go anywhere else."

Good news! I've been given a goldfish for my birthday.
Bad news! I don't get the bowl until my next birthday!

Did you hear about the man who took his dog to the cinema? During a break in the film, the woman sitting in front turned round and said, "I'm surprised that an animal like that should appreciate a film like this."
"So am I," said the man. "He hated the book."

"Why are you crying, little boy?"
"Cos we've just had to have our dog put down!" sobbed the lad.
"Was he mad?" asked the old lady.
"Well, he wasn't too happy about it."

If your cat ate an unripe gooseberry, what would it become?
A sourpuss.

What's white and fluffy, has whiskers
and floats?
A cata - meringue.

What is Dracula's favourite pet?
A Bloodhound

Mum, can I have a puppy for Christmas?
No, you'll have a turkey like everyone else.

Man: Can I have a canary for my
wife please?
Pet Shop Owner: I'm sorry, sir,
we don't do swaps.

What do you do with sick canaries?
Give them tweetment.

Boy 1: I am going to keep this gorilla under my bed.
Boy 2: What about the smell?
Boy 1: He'll just have to get used to it.

**I've been told I have the face of a saint.
Yes, a Saint Bernard.**

Henry: I'd like a pet that I can cuddle.
Henrietta: I'll buy you a piranha fish.

Your beard looks as if it goes to the same vet as my dog.

Fly in the Soup

Waiter, waiter! There are flies on my soup!
Would you prefer soup on your flies, sir?

Waiter, waiter! Is there vegetable soup on the menu?
No, sir, I'm afraid I have a bad cold.

Waiter, waiter! There's a small foot in my soup.
You did order a child's portion, madam.

Waiter, waiter! This lamb is raw!
This is a pet shop, sir.

Waiter, waiter! I ordered fish fingers.
You've brought me fish.
The fingers come as a side dish, sir.

Waiter, waiter! There's a small ram under my table.
You asked for a little butter.

Waiter, waiter! This chicken tastes really tough.
I'm afraid it was eaten by a fox, sir.

Waiter, waiter! There's a hole in my soup bowl.
You did order leak soup, madam.

Waiter, waiter! Why have I got Parmesan cheese on my steak?
You haven't, sir, it's your dandruff.

Waiter, waiter! Why is there an
alarm clock in my meal?
You asked for Chicken Tikka,
I believe.

Waiter, waiter! There's a slug in my salad. I'm sorry, sir, I didn't know you were a vegetarian.

Waiter, waiter! There's a slug in my dinner. Don't worry, sir, there's no extra charge.

Waiter, waiter! There's a slug in my lettuce. Sorry, madam, no pets allowed here.

Waiter, waiter! There's a dead spider in my soup. Yes, madam, they can't stand the boiling water.

Waiter, waiter! There's a fly in my soup. Yes, that's the manager, sir. The last customer was a witch doctor.

Waiter, waiter! My lunch is talking to me!
Well, you asked for a tongue sandwich, sir.

Waiter, waiter! Do you serve snails?
Sit down, sir, we'll serve anyone.

Waiter, waiter! Do you have frogs' legs?
Yes, sir.
Well then, hop into the kitchen for my soup.

Waiter, waiter!
Can I have
frog's legs?
Well, I suppose
you could but you'd
need surgery!

Waiter, waiter! What's this cockroach doing on my icecream sundae?
I think it's skiing downhill.

Waiter, waiter! There's a hair in my soup?
Is it brown or purple? We seem to have lost a monster somewhere.

Waiter, waiter! Could I have a mammoth steak, please?
With pleasure, sir.
No, with ketchup, please.

Waiter, waiter! I can't eat this meat, it's crawling with maggots.
Quick, run to the other end of the table, you can catch it as it goes by.

Waiter, waiter! There's a slug in my lettuce.
Quiet, they'll all want one.

Waiter, waiter! You have your thumb on my steak!
I know sir, I don't want it to fall on the floor again!

Waiter, waiter! This lobster's only got one claw.
It must have been in a fight, sir.
Then bring me the winner.

Waiter, waiter! Why is my apple pie all mashed up?
You did ask me to step on it, sir.

"Waiter, waiter," called a diner
at the Monster Café.
"There's a hand in my soup."
"That's not your soup, sir,
that's your finger bowl."

Waiter, waiter! What is this fly doing in the alphabet soup? Learning to spell, sir.

Waiter, waiter! There's a bird
in my soup.
That's all right, sir. It's bird's
nest soup.

Waiter, waiter! Your tie is in my
soup!
That's all right, sir. It's not
shrinkable.

Waiter, waiter! This coffee
tastes like mud.
I'm not surprised, sir, it was
ground only a few minutes
ago.

Waiter, waiter! Does the
pianist play requests?
Yes, sir.
Then ask him to play
tiddlywinks until I've
finished my meal.

**Waiter, waiter! I don't like
the flies in here.
Well, come back tomorrow,
we'll have new ones by then!**

Waiter, waiter! There's a fly in my strawberry blancmange!
Would you prefer it to be served separately, sir?

**Waiter, I must say that I don't like all the flies in
this dining room!
Tell me which ones you don't like, and I'll chase
them out for you.**

Waiter, waiter!
There's a fly in my soup.
What do you expect for two pounds, sir?
A beetle?

**Waiter, waiter! There's a dead fly
in my soup!
Yes, sir, he's committed insecticide.**

Waiter, waiter! There's a cockroach on my steak.
They don't seem to care what they eat, do they, sir?

**Waiter, waiter! There's a maggot in my salad.
Don't worry, he won't live long in that stuff.**

**Waiter, waiter! There's a
spider in my soup.
It's hardly deep enough to
drown him, sir.**

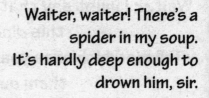

Waiter, waiter! There's a
wasp in my pudding.
So, that's where they go in
the winter.

**Waiter, waiter! There's a fly
in my wine.
Well, you did ask for
something with a little
body, sir.**

Waiter, waiter! What's this dead fly doing on my meat?
I don't know, madam, it must have died after tasting it.

Waiter, waiter! There's a spider in my soup. Send
for the manager!
It's no good, sir, he's frightened of them too.

Waiter, waiter!
There's a mosquito
in my soup.
Don't worry sir,
mosquitoes have
very small
appetites.

Waiter, waiter! There's a beetle
in my soup.
Sorry, sir, we're out
of flies today.

Waiter, waiter! There's a fly in the butter.
Yes, sir, it's a butterfly.

Waiter, waiter! There's a fly in my soup.
Don't panic, sir. I'll call the RSPCA.

Waiter, waiter! There's a fly in my soup!
Don't worry, sir, the spider in your bread will get it.

Waiter, waiter! There's a bee in my
alphabet soup.
Yes, sir, and I hope there's an A, a C,
and all the other letters, too.

Waiter, waiter! There are two flies in my soup.
That's all right, sir. Have the extra one on me.

Waiter, waiter! There's a fly in my soup.
Just a minute, sir, I'll get the fly spray.

Waiter, waiter! There's a fly in my custard.
I know, it's the rotten fruit that
attracts them.

Waiter, waiter! There's a dead
fly in my soup.
Oh, no! Who's going to look
after his family?

Waiter, waiter! What's this
creepy-crawly thing doing
in my lettuce?
I think he's trying to
get out, madam.

Waiter, waiter! What's
this creepy-crawly thing
doing in my dinner?
Oh, that one - he comes
here every night.

Waiter, waiter! What's this
creepy-crawly thing doing
waltzing round my table?
It's the band, sir, it's
playing his tune.

Waiter, waiter! What's this
creepy-crawly thing doing on
my wife's shoulder?
I don't know - friendly little
thing, isn't he?

Waiter, waiter! There's a fly
in my starter. Get rid of it
would you?
I can't do that, sir, he hasn't
had his main course yet.

Waiter, waiter! There's a teeny beetle in my broccoli.
I'll see if I can find a bigger one, madam.

Waiter, waiter! There's a fly in my soup.
Go ahead and eat him. There are plenty more where he
came from.

Sir, you haven't touched your custard.
No, I'm waiting for the fly to stop using it as
a trampoline.

Waiter, waiter! What's this cockroach doing in
my soup?
We ran out of flies.

Waiter, waiter! There's a dead fly
swimming in my soup.
Nonsense, sir, dead flies can't swim.

Waiter, waiter! There's a fly in my soup!
And what's the problem, sir?
I ordered slug soup.

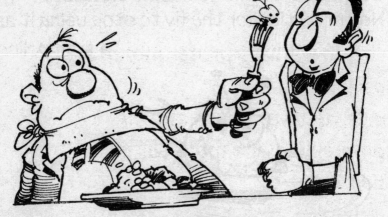

Waiter, waiter! What kind of insect
is this I've found in my dinner?
I don't know, sir, I can't tell one
breed from another.

Waiter, waiter! There's a fly in my bean soup.
Don't worry sir, I'll take it back and exchange it
for a bean.

Waiter, waiter! Did you know there is a fly in my soup?
That's not a fly, sir, it's just dirt in the shape of a fly.

Waiter, waiter! This food isn't fit for a pig!
All right, sir, I'll get you some that is.

Why do waiters prefer monsters to flies?
Have you ever heard anyone complaining of a monster in their soup?

Waiter, waiter! Are there snails on the menu?
Oh, yes, sir, they must have escaped from the kitchen.

Waiter, waiter! Those peas were really hard.
You've just eaten your necklace, madam.

Waiter, waiter! There's a dead beetle in my gravy.
Yes, sir. Beetles are terrible swimmers.

Waiter, waiter! There's a flea in my soup.
Tell him to hop it.

Waiter, waiter! There's a cockroach in my soup!
Yes, sir, the fly is on holiday.

Moaning Monsters

What does a polite monster say when he meets you for the first time?
"Pleased to eat you!"

What is big, hairy and bounces up and down?
A monster on a pogo stick.

On which day do monsters eat people?
Chewsday.

What is a sea monster's favourite dish?
Fish and ships.

What can a monster do that you can't do?
Count up to 25 on his fingers.

How do you know when there's a monster under your bed?
Your nose touches the ceiling.

Why did the monster paint himself in rainbow colours?
Because he wanted to hide in the crayon box.

How do you get six monsters in a biscuit tin?
Take the biscuits out first.

Why did the monster have green ears and a red nose?
So that he could hide in rhubarb patches.

How do you greet a three-headed monster?
Hello, hello, hello.

What aftershave do monsters wear?
Brut.

Why was the big, hairy, two-headed monster top of the class at school?
Because two heads are better than one.

What happened when the monster fell down a well?
He kicked the bucket.

There was a big monster from Leek
Who, instead of a nose, had a beak.
It grew quite absurd
Till he looked like a bird.
He migrates at the end of
the next week.

Why was the monster standing on
his head?
He was turning things over in his mind.

What did the big, hairy monster do
when he lost a hand?
He went to the secondhand shop.

Why did the fat, hairy, drooling monster stop
going out in the sunshine?
He didn't want to spoil his looks.

What happened when the monster stole a bottle of perfume?
He was convicted of fragrancy.

What should you do if a monster runs through your front door?
Run through the back door.

Which is the unluckiest monster in the world?
The Luck Less Monster.

How did the monster cure his sore throat?
He spent all day gargoyling.

There was a big monster called Ned
Who had eyes at the back of his head.
When asked where he was going,
"I've no way of knowing.
But I know where I've been to," he said.

1st monster: I've just changed my mind.
2nd monster: Does it work any better?

Mummy monster: Agatha, how often
must I tell you not to eat with your fingers?
Agatha monster: Sorry, Mum.
Mummy monster: I should think so! Use a
shovel like I do.

Little monster: Mum, I've finished.
Can I leave the table?
Mummy monster: Yes, I'll save
it for your tea.

1st monster: I was in the zoo last week.
2nd monster: Really? Which cage were
you in?

1st monster: Who was that lady I
saw you with last night?
2nd monster: That was no lady, that
was my lunch.

The police are looking for a monster with one eye. Why don't they use two?

There was an old monster with
humps
Who was terribly down in the
dumps.
He was frumpy and grumpy
And jumpy and stumpy
Because of his terrible lumps.

1st monster: What is that son of yours doing these days?

2nd monster: He's at medical school.

1st monster: Oh, what's he studying?

2nd monster: Nothing, they're studying him.

Did you hear about the monster who lived on bits of metal?
It was his staple diet.

Did you hear about the monster who had twelve arms and no legs?
He was all fingers and thumbs.

Did you hear about the monster who had eight arms?
He said they came in handy.

What's a man-eating monster's
favourite book?
Ghouliver's Travels.

What do you call a
one-eyed monster who
rides a motorbike?
Cycle-ops.

What happened to
Frankenstein's monster on
the road?
He was stopped for speeding,
fined £50 and dismantled
for six months.

How did Frankenstein's monster
eat his lunch?
He bolted it down.

What do you call a clever monster?
Frank Einstein.

What do you get if you cross a tall
green monster with a fountain pen?
The Ink-credible Hulk.

What do you get if a huge hairy monster steps
on Batman and Robin?
Flatman and Ribbon.

Two monsters were in hospital and they were
discussing their operations and ailments.
"Have you had your feet checked?"
one asked the other.
"No," came the reply. "They've
always been purple
with green spots."

A mother monster marched her naughty little monster into the doctor's surgery. "Is it possible that he could have taken his own tonsils out?" she asked.

"No," said the doctor.

"I told you so," said the mother monster. "Now, put them back."

Monster: I've got to walk 25 miles home.

Ghost: Why don't you take a train?

Monster: I did once, but my mother made me give it back.

What did Frankenstein's monster say when he was struck by lightning?
Thanks, I needed that.

Did you hear about the monster who was known as Captain Kirk?
He had a left ear, a right ear and a final front ear.

A monster went shopping with sponge fingers in one ear and jelly and custard in the other. "Why have you got jelly and custard sponge in your ears?" asked the shop assistant.
"You'll have to speak up," said the monster. "I'm a trifle deaf."

Why did the monster take his nose apart?
To see what made it run.

What has two heads, three hands, two noses and five feet?
A monster with spare parts.

Superman climbed to the top of a high mountain in the middle of the African jungle. As he reached the summit he found himself suddenly surrounded by dozens of vicious vampires, ghosts, monsters and goblins. What did he say?
"Boy, am I in the wrong joke!"

Robot: I have to dry my feet carefully after a bath.
Monster: Why?
Robot: Otherwise I get rusty nails.

What makes an ideal present for a monster?
Five pairs of gloves – one for each hand.

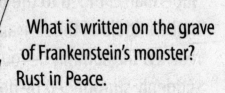

What is written on the grave
of Frankenstein's monster?
Rust in Peace.

What comes out at night and goes munch,
munch, ouch!
A vampire with a rotten tooth.

What would you get if you crossed the Abominable
Snowman and a vampire?
Frostbite.

What's a vampire's favourite sport?
Batminton.

What do vampires cross the sea in?
Blood vessels.

What do vampires have at eleven o'clock
every day?
A coffin break.

Why did the vampire baby
stop having baby food?
He wanted something to get
his teeth into.

Where do vampires go on holiday?
To the Isle of Fright.

Which vampire tried
to eat James Bond?
Ghouldfinger.

What happened at the
vampires' race?
They finished neck and neck.

What do vampires have for
lunch?
Fangers and mash.

Why are vampire families so close?
Because blood is thicker than water.

What is the first thing that vampires
learn at school?
The alphabat.

Why is Hollywood full of vampires?
They need someone to play
the bit parts.

Why do vampires like school
dinners?
Because they know
they won't get
stake.

What is a vampire's
favourite
soup?
Scream
of
tomato.

What is the vampire's favourite breakfast cereal? Ready Neck.

What is the vampire's favourite slogan? Please Give Blood Generously.

Where is Dracula's American office? The Vampire State Building.

Where do vampires keep their savings? In blood banks.

What do popular vampires get? Fang mail.

What type of people do
vampires like?
O positive people.

What's a vampire's favourite
fruit?
Necktarines.

1st vampire: Are you a light sleeper?
2nd vampire: No, I sleep in the dark.

What do vampires play poker for?
High stakes.

Barber: Oops! Sorry, I've just cut your chin.
Vampire: Don't worry, it's not my blood.

Young vampire: Dad, dad, I know what you're getting for your birthday.
Vampire: Really? How?
Young vampire: I felt your presence.

Witch: You should keep control of your little boy. He just bit me on the ankle.
Vampire: That's only because he couldn't reach your neck.

Did you hear about the vampire who got married?
He proposed to his girl-fiend.

Did you hear about the vampire who died
of a broken heart?
He had loved in vein.

Some vampires went to see Dracula. They said, "Drac, we're
going to start a football team."
"Great," he said, "I'll be ghoulie."
They said, "When we've had a bit of practice we'll challenge
the human beings to a game."
Dracula said, "Be careful, the stakes will be high."
They said, "No, we've got this brilliant idea. We'll have these
very long games which'll tire them out. The first half will run
from dusk to midnight and the second half from midnight
till dawn."
Dracula said, "And what happens if it goes to extra time?"

What did the vampire say when he saw
the neck of the sleeping man?
"Ah! Breakfast in bed."

How does a vampire get through life with only one fang?
He has to grin and bare it.

What do you call a vampire who gets up your nose?
Vic.

Where do vampires go fishing?
In the blood stream.

What do you call a short vampire?
A pain in the knee.

What's a vampire's favourite hobby?
In-grave-ing.

Why do vampires never get fat?
They eat necks to nothing.

What airline do
vampires travel
on?
British Scareways.

How does a vampire enter his house?
Through the bat flap.

What sort of group do
vampires join?
A blood group.

Which space movie stars
Count Dracula?
The Vampire Strikes Back.

What's the difference between a vampire with toothache and a rainstorm?
One roars with pain and the other pours with rain.

What's a vampire's worst enemy?
Fang decay.

What do you get if you cross a vampire with a computer?
Love at first byte.

Who are some of the werewolves' cousins?
The whatwolves and the whenwolves.

Did you hear about the comedian who entertained at a werewolves' party?
He had them howling in the aisles.

What do Frankenstein and Boyzone have in common?
They're both made up of four different people.

What is a monster's favourite TV programme?
Beast Enders.

What is the definition of failure?
A vampire with a nosebleed.

What is the two-headed woman's favourite type of joke?
Mummy, Mummy.